CW00411012

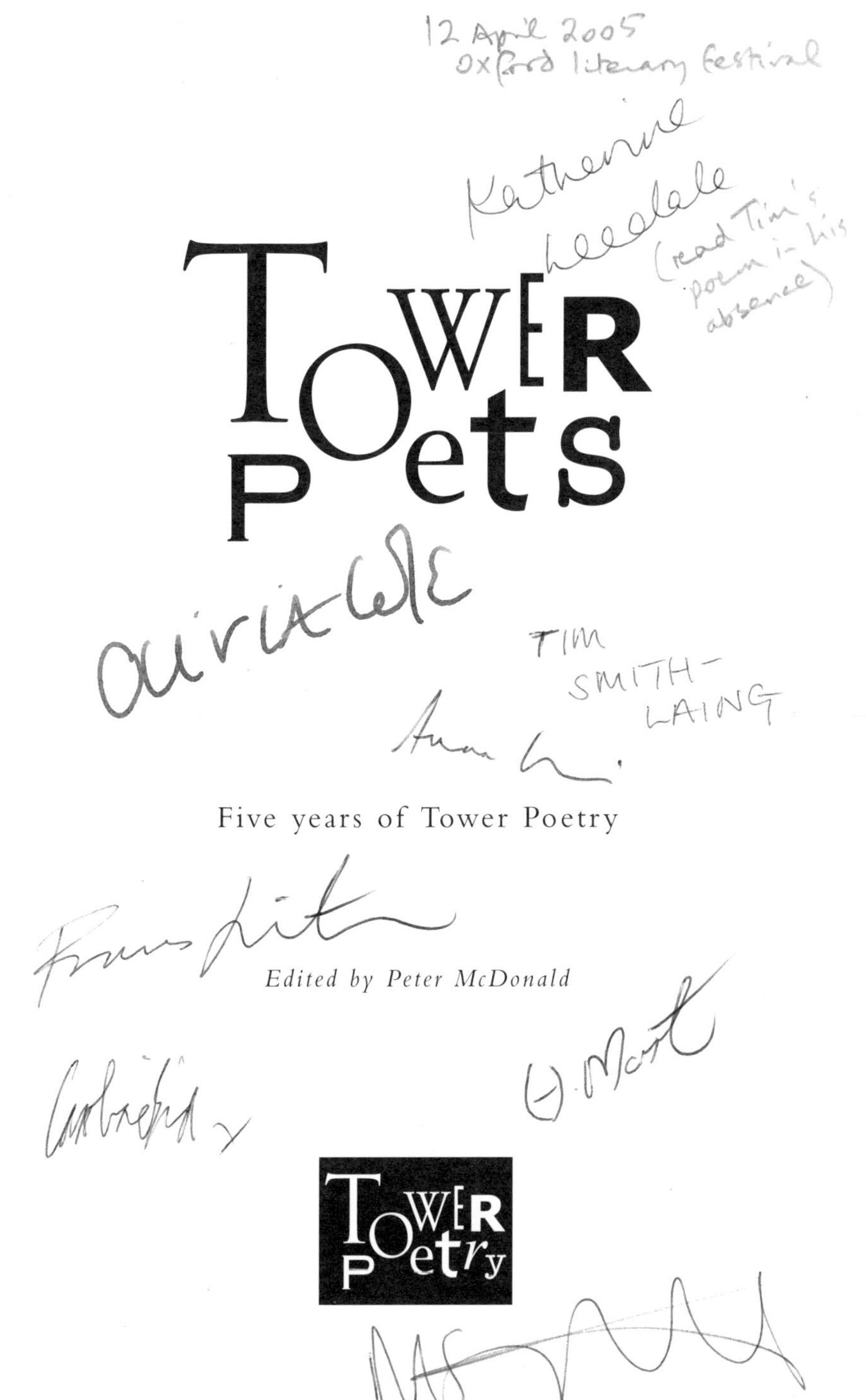

Tower Poets

Five years of Tower Poetry

Edited by Peter McDonald

Tower Poetry

Published by Tower Poetry, Christ Church, Oxford, 2005

A catalogue record for this book is available from the British Library

ISBN 0-9549932-0-9

Printed in the United Kingdom by Hunts

CONTENTS

INTRODUCTION

The seven poets in this book have all been connected, in one way or another, with the work of Tower Poetry. When the late Christopher Tower gave funds to Christ Church, Oxford, to promote the writing and the study of poetry, the several elements that together comprise Tower Poetry came into being: an annual poetry competition for 16-18 year olds, the provision of a Tutorial post in the study and composition of poetry (and part of another in Medieval poetry), as well as a number of initiatives involving the promotion and teaching of creative writing.

After five years, Tower Poetry can now present the work of seven young writers of real promise and achievement. Some have been winners of the competitions; others have taken part in our Summer School; still others have been participants in the regular classes on writing poetry which I have given in the University of Oxford.

All the poets here are different – different from one another, and different from the usual patterns of 'promise' in the world of contemporary British poetry. And they are their own masters: it is a matter of pride that (among other things) Tower Poetry does not promote a house style, whether of poetry or personality, by which to advance a writing career. Poetry, like all art, sits uneasily with establishment: and talk of 'established poets', in the jargon of promotion in contemporary poetry, is bound to be finally self-defeating. Tower Poetry is situated in an Oxford college, one itself established for centuries as a bastion of intellectual independence and creative freedom. In promoting the art of poetry, we are fortunate in being able to let poetry, rather than the agendas of 'promotion', call the shots.

As the work of these poets shows, new talent is always unpredicted – surprising rather than familiar. We are glad to have played some part in promoting this originality and distinctiveness.

Peter McDonald

ANNA LEWIS

Anna Lewis was born in 1984 and she is currently studying archaeology at Manchester University. In 2002, she won the first prize in the Christopher Tower poetry competition, and she was also a winner of the Foyle Young Poets of the Year competition in the same year. Her work has been published in a number of magazines, including Poetry Wales *and* Mslexia.

'Eleanor Morris, 1826' first appeared in Poetry Wales (Vol 40, Issue 2).
'The Verger locks up the cathedral' was first published in Poetry Wales (Vol 40, Issue 3).

ELEANOR MORRIS, 1826

The lights in the sampler room are low,
protective of the girls' long hours framed
dim as bruises on the walls. Eleanor Morris,
twelve years old: I see her pricking her fingers
by gaslight, their tips ten solitaire boards that
sting through her sleep. She watches the sky
peel away from the sea at dawn, sticky patches
of shadow under clouds on the waves: Cardigan
Bay, grey, mirthless, swallows the view. Dank
ships smear the water, industry throttles fields
to the south; cities chew orchards, spit out a
shrivelled new poor. Sulky, twelve; sometimes,
she pricks by design. She concentrates in the
window, stitching letter on letter, pulling tight
the threads, as the landscape grows vague.

THE VERGER LOCKS UP THE CATHEDRAL

In darkness, this place swells like a
rotten fruit. Old incense sickly-sweet,
chapels and cloisters oozing sadness
born of centuries of pain and prayer;
the ghost of each Amen cluttering
their hollow dreams like skulls. Gloom
sniffs at his vestments as he makes his
final rounds, locking doors, switching
off lights. So many penny candles, for so
many frosted souls, are now burnt down,
each alcove and each altar returned to cold.
Sometimes he stops in the main doorway as
he leaves, a steep weariness holding him
still. It is in these moments that he feels
the weight of God, the whole great bulk
of stone slung around his shoulders, like
the train of a young and solemn bride.

THE PACIFIST'S SON

He keeps a list of things he hates beneath the pillow:
gossip, widows; naturally, the Hun. Hymns with no
chorus, doves; his parents' voices after he is in bed -
and this afternoon he'll go home and add the river,
underline it with special malice for its limp tides
and timid banks, for the light dribbled on its
ripples like thin honey, warm, bright and smug.
With higher banks, black water, heroism would be easy -
but he hates excuses more than he hates his father's
nose, mouth, chin in the mirror, his father's eyes,
the stupid tears that clogged them that morning, stumbling
downstairs to breakfast, at the single white
feather slipped under the door.

VISITING HOURS

The glass front of the doll's house
is wrinkled with finger-prints and
grease: but the attendants on their
rounds are elderly, too old to kneel
with Windowlene and sponge, to
watch the slowly looming grey of
their own faces as they clean. Still,

we see where one faint miniature
has tumbled from the parlour wall;
the maid in her yellowed, threadbare
apron; Father's eyes locked to his
paper, world events static as the
clock upon the sloping parlour shelf.

The museum air is dense: sun strains
at the windows, heaving its slabs of
light along the floor. The attendants'
voices creak downstairs, hushed as
though delivering bad news; and the
dim rooms of the doll's house grow

unsettling, the fragile furniture in its
uneasy disarray. We leave more finger-
prints upon the glass and wander on,
still conscious of those small rooms
behind us creeping toward decay; of
those painted mouths, immovable lips,
those bright, unfaltering smiles.

LEAVING

The city spreads like two wings
from the train's thin torso, beating
under watery sun to a half-drawn sky.
While I walked in the streets, shoddy with
smoke and dead leaves, the city's grip
seemed stiff as the pins of a lock

yet now, flattened out to its tips, fraying,
it lifts on sweeps of light: its promises
like so many feathers float free, and the flat
taste of leaving binds my tongue like oil.

HISTORY LESSON

Even two thousand years ago
there were days of this kind:
sullen, unmemorable, trees like
dour ghosts needling a mustard-
tinted sky. Scrappy birds pillage
the fields and woods, the hill-

fort high above the road;
risk the brambles scrawled
sulkily across its dank, half-
flooded ditch. Even on days
like this whole families once
cooked and slept here, harvesting

children, suffering hunger and
grainy cold. If they understood
the strategy of stars, the husky
language between trees, water's
secret swell and fade, were
then they warned that change
would come? Only the sallow

clouds endured it: almost visible,
the curfew of an era strings
across the hill, faint as a cobweb
shifting in and out of light:
secretive, poised soundlessly
between two inauspicious leaves.

THE READING ROOM

It is as though the books themselves
are guilty, chained to shelves behind
an iron gate, like leathery felons in
some dank medieval cell. Scholars
here once trudged from press to
press by candle light, oak boards
mourning beneath their feet. Even
at noon the narrow windows would
catch only shreds of sun, pale, weak
as a shoal of fish, cast out across the
library floor – still, they chained their
books like captured fugitives, as if
they might at any moment lift their
covers, flap away to warmth or light.
Between candle stubs, ink-wells and
damp-bruised walls, they anchored
them: letters languishing in shadow
across the page, enlightenment's small
fire still gasping somewhere deep within.

FRANCES LEVISTON

Frances Leviston was born in Edinburgh in 1982, and later moved to Sheffield. She read English at St Hilda's College, Oxford University, before starting an MA in Creative Writing at Sheffield Hallam University. In 2004, she won Hallam's Ictus Prize, which led to the publication of her first pamphlet, Lighter, *by Mews Press. She is currently working towards a full-length collection.*

'I resolve to live chastely' and 'Unthinkable' first appeared in Lighter *(Mews Press, 2004).*

I RESOLVE TO LIVE CHASTELY

and hurry home, carrying my shoes through empty
precincts as the morning darkens. I thought I could make it
before the wheel of cloud came round
but I am only turning the corner when the heavens begin
to spit like a pack of old women in Salem,

so here I am sheltering under the lintel of St Mary's
church, I'll thank you not to laugh, waiting
for the squall to blow over, with blistered bare feet,
what you get for wearing inhumanly pointed
heels that tie with black ribbon round the ankle

and dancing all night in the name of nothing
noble – not the corps de ballet bleeding splendour
as they assume the positions of true love
for a paying audience, though I did ask
his name, but I've lost it again. The weather vane

pirouettes. I'm thinking of the girl with no breasts
who ate sweet pepper first so she could tell
when to stop throwing up. I want to know who
she imagined was counting, for whom the red stain
was appeasement, for what. I want to know

what keeps me here, back to the grille, straining
for a dry foot of ground, in sight of all those beads
of water sliding down a stem of grass. What else is it
for, my skin, if not this pelting, streaming world?

UNTHINKABLE

I dreamed I was afraid to walk between the tower blocks
that stand on the hill to the west of this city, I was afraid
of the pissed-in stairwells, each a hollow of fallen leaves
and the hanging wires and the ceiling tiles' asbestos
and the clatter and squeak of pushchairs down the walkway

I was afraid of the people inside, trapped like spiders in a sink
neither rescued nor put out of what I imagined to be
their misery, the mean-lipped girls shaking gold charms
and blitz-blonde hair, the men in twisted caps with broken teeth,
with business
to attend to *don't you speak like that to me you slag I'll break your*
fucking jaw

I was afraid of silence, of shrieks banging against each other,
no halfway house between the two, of the organs and the skin, starved
thighs like whippets', all bone and shank, I was afraid of splinters, of
everything
broken but gripping strong as a dead dog's bite, and if there were
no doctors here

but when I woke in the master bedroom I was afraid of nothing
but the cry from the sixth floor harpy-muezzin at dusk, which is the
same
cry that sails from the pigeon coops across the valley
where tenderness is not unthinkable, and I understood the terrible
coughing
in the shut room to be laughter, and that love – love! – answered, came
in from the cold each night, hands shoved in pockets, unspeakable, all
the fiercer for that.

ASHES

Raked-out cool and soft as crumbled silk,
tipping from the hearth's brass spade
on to newsprint; more than expected,
each log finely dense in destruction,
no lighter – the wrapped weight, the moment,
of a baby in your arms – then out
to the garden's bonfire heap
to burn again with the season's wrecked tree,
only wind blows
the folded paper open, and there they go:
grey stream above the winter pond,
purposeful, fanned, reaching-for – a trick
of course, but something held, like dust
that looks to travel up the light.

OTTER FERRY

Never forget we stumbled
up the drunk stone beach, bellies full
of oysters, bread; across the crumbled
concrete bunker's hill

and like two exiled kings
from that high point surveyed
a combed acre of seaweed, stinking
in the dusk; all its betrayed

haul of half-open tins adrift
on the rippled surface, clusters
of midges and sandflies' thrift
busily uncovering the lustre

of waste; how we said
nothing of what we needed to say,
which would rise as the dead's
final airs, ineluctably,

but both palmed a rock
and aimed it at a rusted pipe;
lobbed; fell short; took stock,
and sourced another hope

from what lay at our feet
to try again; how each sad tone
we raised then sounded sweet,
and no shot was in vain.

SIGHT

That winter drift-trapped in the house,
re-learning the furnace of flesh and the endless
tether the mind ranges upon,

I came into the living room and saw
a glass jug suspended in the air, six feet clear
of the carpet, tipped. There were no wires,

no mirror tricks. The whole world hung
on whatever invisible hook or hand
was keeping it tilted, empty, gleaming.

I stepped towards it, as if in a dream. It fell
as rain falls, suddenly out of the sky's
indifference, and shattered at once;

the radio detuned itself, the minister's
pledges slow-flying apart, his spieling
slight and consequent as snow.

JANUARY

for JH

This time, Brighton,
let desire break
against the pier.

Let a man walk
his dog through the ruin
and the dog lift her muzzle
in a forward breeze

and the last lit bulb
on the helter-skelter not revoke
that haven of crash mats
and candy stripe.

Let the loop of element
the element go on

HELEN MORT

Helen Mort is from Derbyshire, and is currently studying Social and Political Science at Christ's College, Cambridge University. She has won the Foyle Young Poets of the Year competition several times, and her work has been published in Dreamcatcher, The Times Educational Supplement, *and* The Rialto. *In 2003, she took part in a performance tour with other writers from the East Midlands, and she continues to be involved with poetry performance in Cambridge.*

THE AGEING OF HARRY HOUDINI

In the mirror each morning
you are not the same,
but should not be afraid;
it is only like the slow
softening of oranges, or the sea
carrying its dead self,
light and wreathed with weeds.

Think how you grew to
fill the shape of every box
they locked you in,
your liquid body rippling,
how you will prise open
your crepe paper skin
and sidle back ten years

to November in a Paris café,
that woman who sighed
a cloud of cigar smoke
between your face and hers,
vanishing before it cleared.

On mornings these days
against the mirror,
we are all perfect forgeries,
waiting for the light to
pan through us.

RISK ASSESSMENT ✓

We started with rain – grey, hair
plastered against our heads -
and you drew for me the heavy lungs
of a valley, filling and swelling
with water, where you had dived,
pulled sideways by current, trying
to touch the river bottom,
and had broken through the surface
with only silt in your eyes,
drowning in the brown water
a story your mother told you
about those lads
the river hugged too tightly.

Opposite 'The Rose and Crown'
the traffic holds its breath for you
and we dodge through cars, drivers
gaping against their windows. You talk
of miracles in the everyday;
the euphoria of an open window,
sunshine unsettling dust across the floor
and the car headlamps flash
across your own small miracle,
the half-way mark of your neck
still bruised with something like luck.

We started with rain,
but then you tell me that
the only thing you've ever wanted
is to make love in a thunderstorm,
watch the clouds crowding in.
The night jostles against my skin,
warning me to assess.
Traffic, with nothing to stay for,
moves on. I am left
to walk the tightrope of your smile
not alone
but by myself.

AN ENGLISHMAN'S GUIDE TO THE EYE OF THE STORM

1. An exquisite geographical phenomenon,
the eye of a hurricane *(n. tropical air disturbance,*
common over warm seas, see Mitch, Mexico,
death.) is caused by air falling
in its centre whilst around it
earth's rotation forces up
strong winds. The unlikely
observer might note the perfect
and somewhat eerie hush
which accompanies the eye -
birds will not sing,
leaves, if left on trees,
will not rustle.

2. Figure of speech, expression
referring to period of
calm *(see tranquillity)*
in which one might imagine
one is through the worst.

3. If finding himself witness
to such circumstances, the prudent
traveller should not become complacent
but take time to check the security
and state of any valuable items,
examine himself for bruising, injury
and unsightly scratches and
prepare for high winds to recommence.

4. Transient happiness -
for clarification, see also
'love'.

LIKE FAITH

You tell me
that when you tire of the logic
of climbing,
your endless spider dance,

you fix your rope to the edge
of a bridge and
dive, headfirst,
swooping underneath
just long enough
to claw a handful of water
and feel it slip through your fingers
like faith.

You smile at the thought,
but to me, the drop
and horizontal pull
were never quite credible,
your pendulum flight
was only a grafted freedom.

Besides, I am too wary for it,
seeing only the thinness of rope,
the shallow-bottomed river
and always, always,
panting over you,
the dark belly of the bridge.

OLIVIA COLE

Olivia Cole is a poet and journalist. Born in Kent in 1981, she read English at Christ Church, Oxford University, where she was awarded the University Gibbs Prize for her thesis on Sylvia Plath. In 2003, as well as becoming an Arvon/Jerwood poetry apprentice, she won an Eric Gregory Award for a first collection, Restricted View.

'The Writer's Dairy' first appeared in the Arvon/Jerwood anthology, Promises to Keep.
'I Can Wait' and 'Ponte Sant'Angelo' first appeared in Magma.
'Breaking the Ice' first appeared in The Liberal.

FLIGHT PATHS

I stood in your shower, how many times?
Well, so many times, pausing always
to look through steam and water and glass
at the city's ineradicable stretch,

washing, wondering how many there must be
to give that flickering orange haze
of glimpsed specifics – rooms, yellow
and stacked, curtains raised to show

silhouettes walking across *their* sets,
drawing, eating, murdering quietly
for all I know or could do -
glances, pauses, halves

of dancing couples illuminated,
until they slip from view to pursue
the routes that have for them,
like us, become routine; their shadow play

hanging on the flick of a single switch,
goodbyes played out elaborately across the hours -
as I would stand, one tentative fingertip
tracking across the centimetres and the miles,

the city a condensed pane of glass
to reach for and write on – traced and known:
as impossible to hold as remembered strings of amber beads,
glinting un-lifted from long-passed market stalls.

THE WRITER'S DAIRY

For my mother

On Amwell Street,
the dairy has been locked up,
abandoned carelessly,
as if an earthquake or volcano
exploded, and not just the decades,
and now all around, slow gentrification.

Damp years of junk mail
load the floor, cool as the milk
and the ice-cream which the signs
still promise can be carried away.
Wholesale boxes of chocolate bars
and crisps are balanced on the till –
brands and packets that till now
I'd never even noticed had disappeared.

Watched by her father,
a girl runs along the street,
he stands at the open door,
I don't know what it is I'm grieving for
or why I feel I should be finding out
who lives here now. It's only
second-hand, that I know
the *Pizza Express* should be the toy shop
or that opposite the dairy, that delicatessen
was never there before.

In the window, the peering face
could almost be a child
who looked just like me,
who'd go in where now there are only
empties and unopened letters,
and dither and queue
and head off at a sprint, past the theatre
and the post office, to find the great grandmother
I never knew.

From St John's Street,
Rosebery Avenue, at dusk,
tiny lights – gold – caught in the trees.
I pass them all the time,
their insistent celebration,
and they always seem half right, just right,
and half all wrong
when on any given day,
I'm years too late for tea,
to stop and get the milk
and cream cakes on my way.

The sharp light dulls;
on the second autumnal day of the year
I take in a gaudy sunset:
pink and orange, bright
because not in spite of the dirt, spilling
beyond the grey, as far as where the city scatters
and someone somewhere still milks cows.

I CAN WAIT

Delete as appropriate

For the last train/plane/boat or bus,
for the last chance plan/lover or saloon,
for my/your last minute change of sex/
heart or mind. He/she/they/we can't/won't

sing/cook/dance or tell the time, but I
can hold on or off, hang about and on,
for the right/wrong time to call/go back/
find my creased/lost/void/no time barred/

expenses spared return. Can laugh/cry
question and plead – seize the platform/
world or stage, tap dance/torture tease
until the audience: enemies/friends/tinkers

tailors/soldiers/sailors laugh/cry/applaud
or get up and leave. Can wait in the light/
dark wings for the right/wrong second/
minute/to find my needle/thread/head/

keys or match, for you to catch my cold/
snow drift/madness/last train home.
Have my ticket/luggage/coffee/name/
unbearable/book/life/magazine. I'm waiting

for the right time to lose my rag/the plot/
my mind, to throw down/up or away my gauntlet/
breakfast/lunch and dinner/his/her home address/
photograph and number, to break your/my neck/

date or fate, to discard in this strange time/city/
world my atlas/A to Z/inaccurate map,
before you can say/understand or underline
a single word.

BREAKING THE ICE

A metallic aftertaste, a gild,
a shine, right or wrong, a glint
of something strong; feet on frost,
an awkwardness that makes
every crunched word loud, every glance
a look; an aperitif cold as arrogance
or a cruel streak. One day we could wake
to a better, warmer kind of gleam

that we'll love more than this askance rude stutter.
And we'll drink deep but knowing all the while
that it tastes nothing like this first stop start
glitter that once gone – twisted, bitter –
there's no way we can demand again,
at least not here and now, with each other.

PONTE SANT'ANGELO

Rome. Pope Clement IX declared Bernini's angels too lovely to be exposed to the weather. Copies were made for the Ponte Sant'Angelo and the originals remained with Bernini's family until 1729, when they were moved to a church. (Spoken by one of the copies.)

I have sisters who live in a church,
dreaming of air, the clinging damp
of low dawn tides. I have sisters, smooth
and white as brides, that the Pope
couldn't bear to let outside. In the sun,
in the wind or the rain, grey as a ghost
and moulded green, I look my age
and watch you walk away. Don't tell me

you don't love them more, but even so,
deep down, come on, you know it's true –
they are, what can I say? Too *good* for you.
Get off the floor. I know it's me,
out here, who makes you shiver.
I've seen the way you cross and re-cross the river.

THE DEEP END

In the frieze, above the view
of the car park, the Athenian torch
is the size of the people, each shade of skin
in the Olympic rainbow scene
as unreal as the next. Below, slung, heavy bunting
separates the crocodiles marched in
to be taught to swim and the routine
of strokes and breaths that trail

in one another's wake. Cluttering up a lane,
I clear my head; the old man I always see
walks the middle stretch of each constitutional length.
The god swimmers, too,
are fading. A quarter mile or half
unspools, and the time it takes
seems impossible to change, however
hard or fast you move towards the sign.

TIM SMITH-LAING

After a highly commended entry in the Christopher Tower poetry competition in 2003, Tim Smith-Laing contributed to the Parachute Silk *collection published as a result of the Tower Summer School that year. He has been published in* Agenda Broadsheet, *and he was one of the Foyle Young Poets of the Year in 2004. He is currently studying English at Pembroke College, Cambridge University.*

UNTITLED

… and who started it,
and grabbed whose clothes,
opened their eyes first to see if the other's were closed,

if you felt like I felt,
or held me like I had to hold what you said,
about kissing my neck when I slept

and at the first leanings in,
and each time since,
if you were kissing or being kissed …

HASTINGS / TYPHOON CLOCK

After the safe rocks and the arcades and the trampolines,
the special train that runs up and down the cliff,
and betting, on every one of those trips,
on machines that race plastic jockeys
on model horses down a six foot track
for 10p bets.

Once I ran backwards away from you both,
along the sea front, to show
how fast, without a slip or a look behind,
watching you all the time,
to see you were watching me,
I could go.

And now I have this clock that you gave me,
from the cockpit of a Typhoon,
that glows in the dark with its radium dial
with twice the normal number of hours
and it still works when you wind it
but only upside down,

which made me laugh when I thought
of the poor pilot and it's no wonder they took it out,
but do you see the sense it makes,
things back to front?
Perhaps, it's not retrospect, but its opposite
looking on all this;

and everything coming is behind us
and we're breaking our necks
to see what we can't,
if we just looked forwards
they would fall into place all the same,
no less unexpected than before,

with no less joy or harm, and no more.
Only I'm not sure it's in me to explain to you,
and I'm not sure you could understand.
The clock confusing friends or winding down too soon,
should have told me perhaps,
or a little boy with grazed hands.

IN TENDERNESS,

each window seals itself with a paper strip kiss,
on every pane two pairs of lips
stretch a tender paper X;

sandbags circle urban ack-ack guns like worm casts
thrown up on grass,
muffle government buildings;

dog-rose tangles of wire
suddenly flower
on our beaches, over anti-tank defences

acronyms multiply,
government departments breed like bacteria.
All this very fast,

then nothing happens.
Eventually, this happens:
Grandad's aircraft carrier is stationed off Scapa Floe,

icicles freeze their falls on every railing,
the crew wrap themselves in layer upon layer,
snow builds

on all the planes, wings
folded, lining the deck, snow builds on everything.
Everything moves slowly and carefully,

but not slowly enough
for Navy stores to catch up:
in case of emergency,

for hand to hand combat
the armoury is filled with pickaxe
handles.

LETTER

Where the live gush or pour, cadavers weep.
My first body made my flesh creep
but I see now how practical: the ease
of dissection after peacetime deaths.

Do you remember my letter?
I poured out in blue ink what they spilt on me
anaesthetised and quiet.
It's not just the warmth, I said, nor the eyes,

but the blood. I don't know how much
the censor took, if his incisions were
kinder than mine; if, when you opened
it up, the ink had run in all the cuts.

THE OBSERVER'S BOOK OF BIRDS

These bright jays are rare jewels set in jet
among the dead.

The crows are a just darker marquetry,
inlaid on dead and dying
blacked up like minstrels by sun and flies.

Larger and blacker still the ravens
have a talent for mimicry
and will repeat the dying pleas and mate for life.

Their calls like shaken matchboxes
the magpies are one for bad and two for good luck -
we call them captain and try to count,

but the calculation of our fortunes is beyond us.
Above us swallows flit and strive,
looking for their own weight in insects.

These bodies have lain themselves down
and lifted up these hungry lives
until we could believe, endless,

the men have shed like snakes
and set their hungry mouths upon the waste.

CAROLINE BIRD

Caroline Bird was born in London in 1986. She has been a winner of the Simon Elvin Young Poets of the Year Awards in 1999 and 2000, she was short-listed for the Geoffrey Dearmer Prize 2001 and was a winner of an Eric Gregory Award in 2002. She won The Peterloo Poets Competition (16-19 year-olds) in 2002, 2003 and 2004, and was a runner-up in the 2004 Christopher Tower poetry competition. She has had poems published in P.N. Review, Poetry Review *and* The North. *She has given readings at The Royal Festival Hall, and the Cheltenham and Ledbury Festivals. Her first collection,* Looking Through Letterboxes, *was published by Carcanet in 2002. She has recently completed a new collection which is due for publication later this year.*

MY THIRD ATTEMPT TO LEAVE

I replaced my legs with charcoal,
leapt, toothless, out the door,
wearing a gut-encrusted hat
I had pulled from a rabbit.
I dragged myself along the motorway,
getting shorter by the mile
and people in the towns
ran out with little plastic buckets
to kindly sell me water for my eyes.
I found myself beside a reservoir,
with pockets full of hard-boiled eggs,
but my reflection was a flash-back
I'd forgotten the night before
I had hollowed out your head,
and slid it slyly over my own.
My name was in your mouth
so I slithered on my stomach
to a public telephone,
you answered in an empty voice,
I hailed the nearest taxi
and I followed the cows back home.

TROUBLE CAME TO THE TURNIP

When trouble came to the village,
I put my love in the cabbage-cart
and we rode, wrapped in cabbage,
to the capital.

When trouble came to the capital,
I put my love in the sewage pipe,
and we swam, wrapped in sewage,
to the sea.

When trouble came to the sea,
I put my love inside a fish
and we flitted, wrapped in fish,
to the island.

When trouble came to the island,
I put my love on a pirate ship
and we squirmed, wrapped in pirate,
to the nunnery.

When trouble came to the nunnery,
I put my love inside a prayer book
and we repented, wrapped in prayer,
to the prison.

When trouble came to the prison,
I put my love on a spoon
and we balanced, wrapped in mirror,
to the soup.

When trouble came to the soup,
I put my love inside a stranger
and we gritted, wrapped in mouth
to the madhouse.

When trouble came to the madhouse,
I put my love on a feather
and we flapped, wrapped in feather,
to the fair.

When trouble came to the fair
I put my love inside a rat,
and we plagued, wrapped in rat,
to the village.

When trouble came to the village,
I put my love in the turnip-lorry
and we sneaked, wrapped in turnip,
a hurried kiss.

CHAINING BIKES TO THIS GIRL IS STRICTLY PROHIBITED

I'm sorry for waking you up twelve times in one night
to polish my flip-flops.
Sorry for comparing your collarbone to a coat hanger.
Sorry for building council-flats on the bones of our bed.
Sorry for sewing up every orifice
then getting all naked.
Sorry for appearing at your door like the resurrection
expecting clean underwear and videos.
Sorry for using your gravestone as a clothes horse.
Sorry for sticking a telescope inside you without asking.
Sorry for eating chocolate in the toilets of your gym.
Sorry for balancing an apple on your head
then shooting you in the cheek.
Sorry for writing the Magna Carta in a made-up language.
Sorry for cutting myself into six bloody chunks
then slamming them all on different trains.
Sorry for unzipping you at school proms
then refusing to be unzipped.
Sorry for raping teenagers in my dreams.
Sorry for strutting down your road with a plague-ridden cart,
piling up the bodies before they were dead.
Sorry for mistaking your eyes for obscene blemishes.
Sorry for leaving you quivering by the fire-escape
while I bonked in a taxi.
Sorry for lining your helter-skelter with sand-paper.
Sorry for urging your therapist to ignore you.
Sorry for telling you I needed space
then playing twister with football teams in bobsleighs.
Sorry for mistaking your veins for poisonous eels.

Sorry for attaching your Chihuahua to an electric whisk.
Sorry for plugging in my headphones at your murder-trial.
Sorry for listening intently to your problems
then fobbing you off with a punch-bag and a drum.
Sorry for making you do back-flips in a small metal box.
Sorry for locking you in a cell with a blind tattooist.
Sorry for eating shit and borrowing your toothbrush.
Sorry for squatting you beneath tables at dinner parties.
Sorry for feeding the left-overs to the dog.
Sorry for fingering your neighbours
then brushing back your hair.
Sorry for loving you with every freckle on my tongue.
Sorry for my bloodless little smile,
sorry for the wet on my face.
Sorry for making the right choice at the right time
in completely good faith.

BREAD

I wish to only need bread.
To love in return for a loaf.
To have a hat. To doff my hat.
I wish to have a friend called Larry.
I wish me and Larry could sit
quietly and eat our bread.
Slowly, with our fingers,
or with big chunky forks.
To arrange my bread
on the floor and sing to it.
Sing to my bread.
Eat my bread in little chews.
No conversation. No contact.
Just bread and looking out of windows.
Thinking of bread. I wish
to cherish you, or Larry, or anyone
with a blind bread love
that is fresh and plain
and steady on the stomach.
A love that never hurts or changes.
A love based on bread.
Giving bread, receiving bread,
bread fluffing down from the sky.
I wish to only need bread.
I wish to be bread.

MATTHEW SPERLING

Born in 1982, Matthew Sperling grew up in Meopham in Kent, and studied English at Keble College, Oxford University. He currently studies contemporary poetry as a postgraduate at Corpus Christi College. He has won awards for his poetry and critical writing including the Lord Alfred Douglas Prize, the Charles Oldham Shakespeare Prize, and two Gibbs Prizes. He has worked variously as a seller of bonsai trees, a dictionary assistant for an academic publisher, and a member of the Crackhorse Productions theatrical troupe, devising and performing two shows at the Edinburgh Fringe. It was while doing this that he met artist Elizabeth Hancock, to whom he became married in March 2005.

TRADESCANT'S RARITIES

This traffic. These arrivals. Every atom (which is the smallest
indivisible unit of time) shows cars, green lights, the street, that blanket
I stumbled when I saw

—that red, discarded pair of rubber gloves
for spooling bitumen or tarmacadam
lying in the gutter   looks
like a dead bird smashed on a window,
almost

Nothing
is apropos: flux and reflux come and dissolve, in-
solubly
while John Tradescant, the keeper
of gardens, vines and silkworms, the *senex*
puerilis, the boyish
old man in his finery,
hoarding his queer *naturalia* (all these
minimal lilies, the hawk-gloves of monarchs, Chief Powhatan's mantle,
encephalitic or Siamese foetuses pickled in vinegar, labelled
LUNATIC BABY), tells us *Natura nihil*
agit frustra, Nature
does nothing in vain. From the Ark,

at least a nucleus of the less perishable
items has survived:

broken jars, fragments
of crockery, ampoules of morphine, clumps
of congealed paint

—uncanny, faced with this mockery (say it, *a marriage of monkeys*), where the excess of the actual might
be reduced

might be calcined: to quicklime,
to vapour. Where objects refuse to be held,
they won't, they won't be themselves: random data, their qualia,

streaming
slant-wise around me, now troping themselves in the

turning confection.

John Tradescant (ca.1580-1638) came from Meopham in Kent – the village I grew up in – to be the greatest collector, traveller and naturalist of his age, gardener to Charles I. Tradescant the Younger (1608-62) succeeded him. This small anthology of disorder (*anthology*: 'a gathering of flowers') has been curated in the spirit of the Tradescants' collection of rarities. 'The Ark' in Lambeth passed to Elias Ashmole and so formed the basis for the Ashmolean Museum, Oxford. Some of its rarities find their way into that poem, along with some I've made up. The contents of this cabinet of curiosities were written here and there over the last five years. Exhibited: insects and arachnids under glass (a disclaimer: no animals were harmed in the making of these poems). Flowers, tinfoil, quotations. A poem conjoining nine sentences from *Madame Bovary* to make a miniature surrealist cartoon. A presentably quatrained gap-year travelogue ('The Writer on Holiday'). Fragments of love, domestic life, with pronouns and genders interchangeable. A post-romantic idyl, dead leaves and all, in a refrain-stanza derived from a nineteenth-century example. Are you kidding me? Well, yes and no. It seems to me poetry needn't pretend not to be ludicrous, prodigal, inordinate. But at the same time I want to say I meant every word that follows, once.

Reading by lamp-light at night I become aware of a moth – *click-click-click-click-click* – in the darkened room. He settles on my book:
Look at him, hovering like a thought
held, over the page—that fragile trust…
then snap the book shut.
Open. Finely wrought
from the brown body, the broken scrap of wing,
the filmy dust is golden now; is gold-dust—
transfigured, splendid; symbolizing nothing.

a guy at a party
tells you you've got
'such a weak handshake
boneless the weakest
in all Christendom'

You're stung
You'll show him
weak huh?
touché
I'll take his sweaty
palm and squeeze
hard
the bones
will click in place
crinkle
like tinfoil

then let go and slack
his hand will drop
in pain between
his thighs

and no-one will go
mano à mano against me
again

(*mano*
à mano meaning
'man to man')

As if a bee were author of himself,
making a beeline
—as if the fine
indefinable tact
of the bee (or not a bee) here trapped
in a beer-glass
(like a snow-storm a Christmas gift)
shaking its quiddity
against the contained air
to knock itself out

—as if such stamina
humming like a pylon
pressed to the glass as if
to a yielding stamen

could free itself   and fly
            freely simply being
itself   directed   clarified
            to a black-yellow
speck of quick light like a bullet

            out of the body

—but it seems this bee's stuck
                                        being accustomed
complected   costumed

—blooming buzzing   camp   confused
            with himself

—I hate him
            this pompom this bauble
of fat wax and honey

(I can't stop staring at him)

—and rage and hurt and want and baffled desire
with no sting in the tail

While I was writing… I had standing on my desk an empty beer glass with a scorpion in it. From time to time the creature became sickly; then I used to throw a piece of soft fruit to it, which it would then furiously attack and empty its poison into; then it grew well again…

1

Something furious in it,
what could be
a pair of swollen figs butted
end to end, and angry

—when the warm and sectioned
body grows sickly caught
in a beerglass
a specimen jar
something furious happens
to the apple
that he throws:

(hold there: watch, and wait: suspended, maybe the moment
can be put off: no, watch, the scorpion)

as he cleaves
to the apple
the poison
is emptied
in jerks,
injected

to the sleepy flesh.

He finishes,

twitching,

backs off

and rests;

the specimen deposited,

necrotic,

he recovers.

2

Repeat the pattern. The scorpion
won't tire, keeping
restive and wary, till a new fruit
brings a new
awareness of health, till
all of his bad
poisoned self, his lonely
impulse of disgust
is vented, eased.

The prose quotation at the head of that poem comes from a letter of Henrik Ibsen's. His next sentence asks, 'Is there not something similar to that about us poets?' One of the things I hope my poem suggests is that the answer to Ibsen's question might be 'No'.

A form for holding vacancy in,
or plenitude out; a form to brace
the knees chest-tight under the chin,
with strappings taut across the face;

a form weaving separate parts
into its fabric, bound by a hem;
to stop the body from flying apart
limb by limb, member by member

Thus sung or would or could or should have sung:

'Down past that tree-lined stretch of track
  that follows alongside the stream
without a hint of turning back
  (as if caught in a dream),
without a hint of turning back
our heavy legs, we slowly trek

Up to the woodlands where leaves lie
  clotting the mud they've fallen on
like memories which might half-die
  but aren't completely gone
(like memories which might half-die
for both of us), where you and I

Decide "to talk": you've been assizing
   all the problems we've disguised;
you've had enough of compromising
   and being compromised;
you've had enough of compromising,
you say—and now I face your rising

Anger and boredom and revolt
   at all the things we are together;
and know we can't be "more adult",
   caught idling by the river;
and, no, we can't be "more adult";
and, no, that's all my fault.'

The word *pastiche* comes from French via Italian *pasticcio*, from late Latin *pasta*, 'paste'. A critic writes: 'Pastiche is, like parody, the imitation of a peculiar mask, speech in a dead language; but it is a neutral practice of such mimicry... devoid of... any conviction that alongside the abnormal tongue you have momentarily borrowed, some healthy linguistic normality still exists.' So this set of pastiches – this collection of stage-pastes – shows a young *curioso* trying to become a *virtuoso* in as many abnormal tongues as he can ply ('he' here meaning me), but being curious too at that word 'healthy', what it might mean to have an 'unhealthy' interest in language, where the cordon might be. *Cordon*, n., from French again: 'A guarded line between infected and uninfected districts, to prevent intercommunication... *lit.* and *fig.*' Lit. and fig., how can the lines of a poem then risk being unguarded?

...I'll say something domestic: how softly foil folds
in on itself, beautiful. Standing in the kitchen
at the kitchen sink you rock
back and forth gently
from toe to heel with your eyes closed, crushing a wodge
of kitchen foil in your fist to a ball, like a man
in grip of a breakdown

I need things – everything – to be seen
afresh, to be fresh. It's such an expansive field
I can't take a breath

You have me by the hand
and we walk, untalking, the length of the narrow garden
while I count the paces in my head, and you, you're thinking
whatever you might be thinking.
The trunk is felled, the patio
water-blasted, all pristine;
the Gute Nacht delphinia, rising
purple and fastidious;
the narcissi,
the sunlight.
Where the garden
chokes, deranged
flower-arrangements give back
a reflection. The world won't settle as
or for itself. Things are divorced. You tell me
what I want
to avoid some things
which you won't let me, you

mistake me, I'm just
a sucker with no self-esteem
Can't we
go to bed and mend our wanting
heads and bodies now
with vinegar and brown paper
like before?
The flowerbeds stretch down in shelves to the lawn
The narcissi, the blue delphinia
sway, and prance, and preen themselves like dolphins.
I am myself
a part from this
demoralised
landscape. The period
is ended, period...

The coach took seventy breakneck minutes, leading
away from Prague, past fields of cars & stones.
(The woman next to us was breast-feeding.)
We were off to see the church covered in bones.

We followed the signs out to the ossuary.
I scanned the leaflet, afraid the place was full,
& tried the German: UNSTERBLICH IST DIE
GERECHTIGKEIT. "Righteousness is Immortal".

(For *Immortal*, the erratum read
Immoral.) Inside, we saw the femurs set
in cross-shapes; pelvis-flowers in a bed
of horny ribs. I looked back to the leaflet:

maybe some ancient plague had overflowed
the town with corpses, till some crafty nun
had thought of doing this. The tour guide showed
a chandelier made all of bones, with one

giggling skull sporting a cap which said
NIKE. (Leaflet: "Konserve respekt to the dead.")

A FETISH

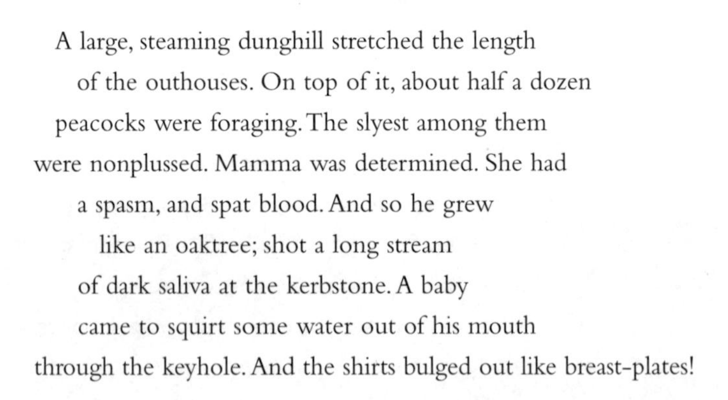

A large, steaming dunghill stretched the length
of the outhouses. On top of it, about half a dozen
peacocks were foraging. The slyest among them
were nonplussed. Mamma was determined. She had
a spasm, and spat blood. And so he grew
like an oaktree; shot a long stream
of dark saliva at the kerbstone. A baby
came to squirt some water out of his mouth
through the keyhole. And the shirts bulged out like breast-plates!

The song, the varied action of the blood

Burn out this sepsis, trace
  the line the vein
describes until it reaches
  lymph-nodes, lodes
of crude health to be exploited,
  worked, refined,
now filigreed, now hammered
to a *fleur-de-lys* ringing with good
  broken music, veins and chambers
coursing with an elixir – Lucozade
  Sport – oh my chevalier!
      The moment hangs, prolonged
in the failing body. Returns
  diminish; the fire
gutters and recedes. The song
takes as its measure what the song
  desires.